Spellathon
Book 2

www.pegasusforkids.com

© **B. Jain Publishers (P) Ltd.** All rights reserved. No part of this book may be reproduced, stored in a retrieval system or transmitted, in any form or by any means, mechanical, photocopying, recording or otherwise, without any prior written permission of the publisher.

Published by Kuldeep Jain for B. Jain Publishers (P) Ltd., D-157, Sector 63, Noida - 201307, U.P.
Registered office: 1921/10, Chuna Mandi, Paharganj, New Delhi-110055

Printed in India

CONTENTS

A AND B 4

C AND D 6

E AND F 8

G AND H 10

I AND J 13

K AND L 15

M AND N 18

O AND P 20

Q AND R 22

S AND T 24

U, V AND W 27

X, Y AND Z 29

SPECIAL SOUND WORDS 31

WORD POWER 33

APPENDIX: SIGHT WORDS 35

ANSWERS 36

A AND B

1. Match the following:

   a. Arrow

   b. Bird

   c. Apple

   d. Baby

   e. Bee

2. Fill in the blanks:

   | Artist | Bell | Ball | Ant |

   a. This is a _____    b. This is a _____

   c. This is an _____    d. This is an _____

Date: _____   Teacher's Signature: _____

3. Help Anna unjumble the words given in brackets and then fill in the blanks:

   1. The sky is b __ u __ (lbue)

   2. We all have two a __ m __ (smra)

   3. I ride a b __ __ e (kibe)

   4. I play with a b __ l __ (llab)

   5. My a __ e (gae) is 6 years.

4. Tick (✓) the correct words:

a. 	Ape		Ant	
b. 	Arrow		Aeroplane	
c. 	Bed		Boat	
d. 	Black		Brown	

Words to Remember

 About, Act, Add, Aeroplane, Age, Aim, Airy, Ant, Ape, Apple, Arms, Arrow, Artist, Ash, Ask, Axe

 Baby, Ball, Band, Bang, Barn, Beak, Bean, Bear, Bed, Best, Bike, Bird, Black, Blue, Boat, Bring, Brown, Burn, Buy

Teacher's Signature: _____ Date: _____

C AND D

1. Look at the pictures and choose the correct spellings:

a. Dack

   Duck

   Dek

b. Cow

   Crawe

   Crow

c. Date

   Dent

   Data

d. Dorm

   Dram

   Drum

e. Cake

   Caik

   Cawek

f. Cold

   Clod

   Cloud

g. Doll

   Dol

   Doal

h. Carr

   Care

   Car

Date: _____

Teacher's Signature: _____

2. Circle the things that begin with the letter C:

3. Look at the pictures and fill in the blanks:

   a. This is a _____ (dog/cat).

   It runs to Sam when he _____ (cold/calls).

   b. This is a _____ (drum/cup).

   Sam will _____ (eat/drink) his milk when it is _____ (cold/could).

Words to Remember

C Cage, Cake, Call, Cane, Cape, Car, Care, Cell, Chair, Child, Cloud, Coat, Cold, Come, Cool, Cow, Craft, Crow, Cup

D Damp, Dance, Dare, Date, Days, Dear, Deer, Dirt, Does, Dog, Dolls, Door, Down, Drum, Duck

Teacher's Signature: _____ Date: _____

E AND F

1. Name the following:

   | Ear | Eye | Frog | Egg | Flag | Fish |

   a. _____ b. _____ c. _____

   d. _____ e. _____ f. _____

2. Change the underlined letters to make new words:

   Remember, you can replace the underlined letter with either e or f. In some words, both e or f can be used, while in others only one of these can make a new word. The first one has been done for you:

   a. <u>C</u> A T   E A T / F A T

   b. <u>S</u> L A G   _ L A G

   c. B <u>A</u> D   B _ D

   d. B <u>O</u> A T   B _ A T

   e. <u>O</u> V E R   _ V E R

   f. <u>D</u> O G   _ O G

   g. B <u>O</u> N D   B _ N D

   h. L I <u>N</u> T   L I _ T

Date: _____   Teacher's Signature: _____

3. Choose the correct answers from the box.

a. Suri has _____ dolls.

b. Katy has _____ cats.

c. Lenny has _____ books.

Box: Four, Five, Six, Eight, Nine

4. How many new words can you make from the word given below?

ELEPHANT

One has been done as an example. Try to make at least four more words.

HELP _____   _____   _____   _____

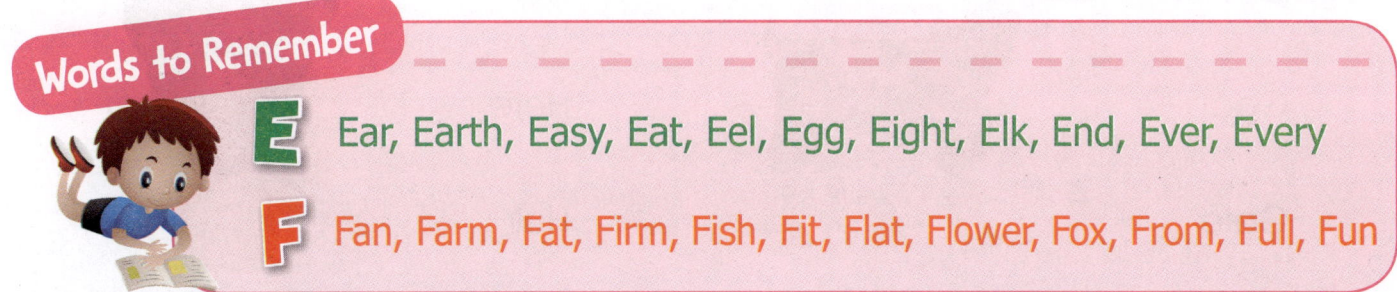

Words to Remember

E — Ear, Earth, Easy, Eat, Eel, Egg, Eight, Elk, End, Ever, Every

F — Fan, Farm, Fat, Firm, Fish, Fit, Flat, Flower, Fox, From, Full, Fun

Teacher's Signature: _____   Date: _____

G AND H

1. Fill in the blanks to complete the names of the following:

   a. Gril

   Girl

   Goil

   b. Hors

   Hours

   Horse

   c. Game

   Gime

   Gaim

   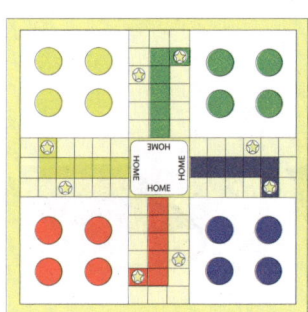

   d. Haus

   House

   Hause

   e. Hand

   Hound

   Hide

   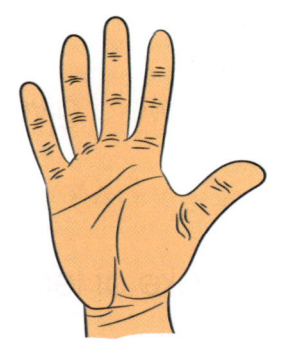

   f. Gars

   Grass

   Grace

   g. Gout

   Goat

   Gote

   h. Hair

   Here

   Heir

Date: _____   Teacher's Signature: _____

2. Look at the picture and find out the correct words. The answers have been jumbled up:

a. This is a _____ (hsoue).

b. The roof of the house is _____ (rgeen).

c. The house is on top of a _____ (lihl).

d. Sima is giving Mira a _____ (guh).

e. Ram is eating _____ (gapres).

Teacher's Signature: _____ Date: _____

3. Choose the correct words to fill in the blanks:

> Games   Horns   Gifts   Grass   Hands

a. A goat has two _____

b. It likes to eat _____

c. I clap with my _____

d. I play _____ with my friends.

e. I got many _____ on my birthday.

4. Circle the spellings that are not correct:

a. Hat    b. Gerl

c. Horce    d. Hero

e. Goose    f. Heal

Words to Remember

 Gain, Games, Gear, Gem, Gets, Girl, Goat, God, Gone, Got, Green

 Habit, Had, Hands, Has, Hat, Hay, Heal, Heat, Heel, Her, Him, Hole, Hope, Horns, Horse, Hot, House, How

Date: _____   Teacher's Signature: _____

I AND J

1. Use the first letter of the name of each picture to make a new word. The first one has been done for you:

a.    =

   J   A   R   =   JAR

b.  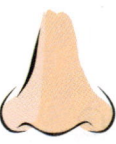  =

   ☐   ☐   ☐   =   ☐

c.    =

   ☐   ☐   ☐   =   ☐

d.     =

   ☐   ☐   ☐   ☐   =   ☐

e.       =

   ☐   ☐   ☐   ☐   ☐   ☐   =   ☐

Teacher's Signature: _____   Date: _____

2. Find the following words in the wordgrid given below:

I	I	C	I	C	L	E	I	I
G	N	L	R	N	L	E	I	V
L	K	J	E	L	L	Y	J	Y
O	P	J	L	U	D	J	O	W
O	O	A	A	J	D	A	K	J
J	T	I	N	S	I	D	E	U
E	N	L	D	J	D	E	R	G
T	J	A	W	J	A	M	O	I
I	S	L	A	N	D	J	E	O

Jelly   Igloo
Inside   Joker
Jug   Jail
Jet   Jaw
Jade   Jam
Inkpot   Icicle
Island   Ivy
Ireland

3. These words are missing a letter and you have two choices: I and J. So take your pick and find the right fit!

   a. M A G __ C   b. __ A C K E T
   c. B __ G   d. L __ K E
   e. __ O K E   f. __ U M P

4. How many words can you make out of the following word?

   JOYFULLY

   _____   _____   _____   _____

Words to Remember

I — Ice cream, Ice, Icicle, Igloo, Ill, Inkpot, Inside, Into, Island, Ivy

J — Jade, Jail, Jar, Jaw, Jeep, Jelly, Jet, Job, Jog, Joy, Joyful, Jug, Jump, Jungle, Just

Date: _____   Teacher's Signature: _____

14

K AND L

1. Look at the pictures and circle the right spellings:

a. Lion
   Loin
   Layn

b. Nife
   Knife
   Knaif

c. Kait
   Kite
   Kayt

d. Lake
   Leak
   Leik

e. Kei
   Keigh
   Key

f. King
   Keng
   Keing

g. Lump
   Lamp
   Lemp

h. Leg
   Lug
   Log
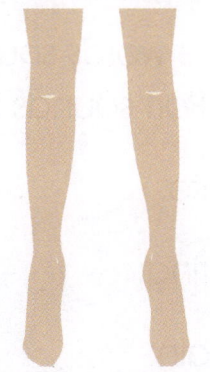

Teacher's Signature: _____   Date: _____

2. The following words have been jumbled up. Can you find out what the correct words are? Remember, all the words begin with the letters K or L.

    a.   Laef

    b.   Laep

    c.   Kiettn

    d.   kiwi

    e.   Kdi

    F.   Lmae

3. Tick (✓) the words that you think rhyme with the given words:

(Some words sound similar to other words. For example: Thing sounds like Sing, and Part sounds like Cart. These are all called Rhyming Words.)

a. Bite:	Kite	Light	Kit
b. Bring:	Long	King	Lane
c. Pain:	Kind	Lane	Line

Date: _____   Teacher's Signature: _____

d. Song:	Long	Kite	King
e. Hit:	Lit	Kit	Lot
f. Sleep:	Leap	Keep	Lope
g. Make:	Like	Lake	Key
h. Wife:	Life	Loaf	Knife

4. Choose the correct words to fill in the blanks:

   a. A baby cat is called a _____ (kangaroo/kitten)

   b. I like to _____ (lick/lump) an ice-cream.

   c. We use a _____ (knife/key) to open a lock.

   d. We can get a _____ (loud/loaf) of bread from the Baker's shop.

   e. We should look _____ (left/lift) and right before crossing the road.

   f. Our _____ (legs/lungs) help us to breathe.

Words to Remember

K Kangaroo, Keen, Keep, Key, Kick, Kid, Kind, King, Kit, Kite, Kitten, Kiwi, Knife

L Lake, Late, Leaf, Leave, Left, Legs, Lick, Lid, Lift, Light, Like, Lime, Link, Lion, Lips, Load, Loaf, Long, Low, Lungs

Teacher's Signature: _____   Date: _____

M AND N

1. Use the first letters of the following to make a new word:

    =

a. ☐ ☐ ☐ ☐ = ▭

 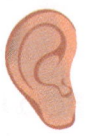   =

b. ☐ ☐ ☐ ☐ = ▭

    =

c. ☐ ☐ ☐ ☐ = ▭

    =

d. ☐ ☐ ☐ ☐ = ▭

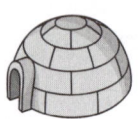    = **9**

e. ☐ ☐ ☐ ☐ = ▭

Date: _____   Teacher's Signature: _____

2. Choose the correct answers:

   a. It is very dark during _____. (night/day)

   b. Twelve o'clock in the day is also called _____. (moon/noon)

   c. Birds lay eggs in their _____. (neck/nest)

   d. At night we can see the stars and _____. (mine/moon)

3. Solve the jumbles and name the following:

   a. NGMAO   __ A N __ O   (Hint: A sweet fruit)

   b. SINOE   __ O __ S __   (Hint: Loud sounds)

   c. LAIN N   __ I __   (Hint: Used to hang up pictures)

   d. VOMIE   __ O V __ __   (Hint: Films)

4. How many words can you make using the letters given along side? Remember to use the alphabet M in every word:

   _____ _____ _____

   _____ _____

   Letters: E, T, M, L, A

Words to Remember

M Mad, Made, Magic, Maid, Man, Mango, Maple, Market, Mash, Mask, May, Meal, Mean, Meant, Meat, Mice, Middle, Milk, Mind, Mine, Mint, Mist, Mix, Money, Moon, More, Most, Mother, Mouse, Mug, Music

N Nail, Near, Neat, Neck, Nest, Net, Never, New, Next, Nib, Nice, Night, Nine, Nip, Noise, None, North, Nose, Now, Null, Numb, Nun, Nuts

Teacher's Signature: _____   Date: _____

O AND P

1. Use the clues to solve the crossword:

Down:

a.    b.    c.

d.    e.

Across:

c.    d.    e.

2. Fill in the blanks with the right words:

   a. The farmer has two _____ (oxen/ocks)

   b. My brother is a _____ (peint/painter)

   c. I like the colour _____ (penk/pink), but my friend likes the colour _____ (orange/orunje)

   d. My dog hurt his _____ (pie/paw)

   e. I don't like to eat _____ (onions/onyuns)

3. Change the underlined letters to make new words:
   Remember, you can replace the underlined letters with either O or P.

   a. M A R K   __ A R K

   b. C A R   __ A R

   c. N E A R   __ E A R

   d. T A K E   T A __ E

   e. N E T   N __ T

   f. B A R N   B __ R N

Words to Remember

O Oar, Odd, Odour, Often, Oil, Okay, Omit, Onion, Only, Open, Oral, Orange, Our, Outside, Oval, Owl, Own, Oxen

P Pace, Pad, Paid, Pain, Paint, Painter, Pan, Pane, Pant, Park, Part, Patch, Paw, Pay, Pear, Pearl, Peel, Peer, Pen, Pencil, Pest, Pet, Pig, Pinch, Pine, Pink, Pitch, Plane, Playing, Please, Pocket, Point, Poke, Pony, Poor, Pot, Pour, Powder, Push, Put

Teacher's Signature: _____   Date: _____

Q AND R

1. Circle the things that begin with R:

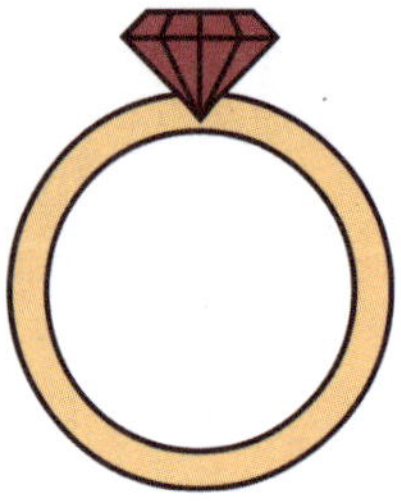

2. Choose the correct words to fill in the blanks:

   a. We should be _____ (quiet/quote) while praying.

   b. My pet _____ (ribbit/rabbit) likes carrots.

   c. The moon is _____ (round/rewind) in shape.

   d. The hut is by the side of the _____ (rover/river).

   e. A female ruler is called a _____ (quilt/queen)

Date: _____   Teacher's Signature: _____

3. Find the following words in the word grid:

Quilt   Quiet   Ring   Reading   Ribs   Rags   Rash   Realise   Quest

S	U	R	A	G	S	H	R
Q	R	I	B	S	L	Q	A
U	E	N	Q	I	Q	U	S
E	A	G	U	Q	U	I	H
S	L	T	R	S	I	E	S
T	I	Q	U	I	L	T	S
U	S	L	R	E	T	T	Q
R	E	A	D	I	N	G	Q

Words to Remember

Q Quarter, Queen, Quest, Question, Quick, Quiet, Quill, Quilt, Quit, Quite, Quiver

R Rabbit, Raft, Railing, Rain, Rainbow, Raise, Raise, Raw, Read, Ready, Real, Red, Rest, Ribs, Right, Ring, Ripe, Rise, River, Robber, Robe, Robot, Room, Rope, Rowing, Rubber, Running, Rush

Teacher's Signature: _____   Date: _____

S AND T

1. The names of the following things start with either S or T. Place them in the correct column:

S	T

Date: _____ Teacher's Signature: _____

2. What's in the box?

   a. Seven Ships

   b. Ten Trees

   c. Six Swans

   d. Three Toffees

3. Try to make as many new words as you can from the following. Remember, each word must have at least three letters.

   a. SUNSHINE   : _____

   b. TRANSPORT : _____

Teacher's Signature: _____   Date: _____

4. Make two words that begin with the following letters. The first one has been done for you:

   a. T A ___ ___   TALL, TAIL
   b. S T ___ ___   _____, _____
   c. T E ___ ___   _____, _____
   d. T H ___ ___   _____, _____
   e. SH ___ ___   _____, _____
   f. SE ___ ___   _____, _____
   g. TO ___ ___   _____, _____

5. Unscramble the following:

   a. ITREG   _____
   b. ATLBE   _____
   c. USGRA   _____
   d. TOSOL   _____

Words to Remember

S — Sack, Said, Salt, Same, Saw, Scare, Scene, Score, Sea, Seat, See, Sell, Send, Sew, Ships, Single, Six, Soap, Sort, Soup, South, Spell, Stair, Star, Stare, Still, Stool, Stop, Sugar, Summer, Sunday, Swans, Swim

T — Table, Tall, Tame, Tape, Tasty, Teach, Tell, Test, That, Thing, This, Those, Three, Tick-Tock, Tiffin, Tiger, Tile, Till, Tilt, Time, Tin, Tip, Tire, Toffee, Top, Toy, Train, Trap, Tree, Two

Date: _____   Teacher's Signature: _____

U, V AND W

1. Look at the pictures and circle the right spellings:

   a. Umbarl
      Umberela
      Umbrella

   b. Vase
      Vise
      Vace

   c. Wach
      Watch
      Wotch

   d. Vegetable
      Vegitabel
      Vagetible

   e. Webb
      Wabe
      Web

   f. Winter
      Want
      Warmer

   g. Unifront
      Uniform
      Unicorn

   h. Whomen
      Woomin
      Woman

   i. Vulture
      Voltore
      Vulcher

   j. Unkle
      Uncel
      Uncle

Teacher's Signature: _____   Date: _____

2. Solve the jumble and fill in the blanks:

> WATER VALLEY USE VIOLIN WOOL UNDER
> WEST VOWELS UNTIL VISIT VASE

a. My sweater is made of _____ (LOWO)

b. I slept _____ (UTNLI) 7 o'clock.

c. The sun sets in the _____ (SEWT)

d. Tia put flowers in the _____ (VSEA)

e. The cat was _____ (NUDRE) the table.

f. The _____ (VLLEAY) was full of flowers.

g. I went to _____ (VSITI) my sister.

h. I do not know how to _____ (SUE) a scale.

i. Mary is learning to play the _____ (LIVION)

j. I wash my hands with soap and _____ (TEWAR)

k. A,E,I,O,U are called _____ (OVWESL)

Words to Remember

 Umbrella, Uncle, Under, Undo, Uniform, Unsafe, Until, Up, Urn, Use, Useful

 Vain, Valley, Van, Vase, Vat, Vegetable, Very, Vest, Video, View, Violet, Violin, Voice, Vote, Vowels, Vulture

W Wag, Wait, Wake, Was, Wasp, Wasp, Waste, Watch, Water, Web, Went, West, Whale, What, When, Where, While, Who, Wild, Win, Wind, Winter, Wire, Wise, Wolf, Woman, Wood, Wool, Word, Wore

X, Y AND Z

1. Unscramble the words to name the picture:

| YELLOW ZIP X-MAS YOLK ZEBRA XEROX ZIGZAG YACHT |

a.
AYCTH

b.
BEZRA

c.
LOKY

d.
MXSA

e.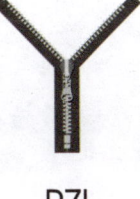
PZI

f.
RXEOX

g.
LOYLEW

h.
GZIGZA

Teacher's Signature: _____   Date: _____

2. Each of the following words is missing a letter. The missing letter could be X, Y or Z. Fill in the right letter to make the word:

   a. E__act   (Exact/Eyact/Ezact)

   b. Ever__   (Everx/Every/Everz)

   c. A__e   (Axe/Aye/Aze)

   d. Ama__e   (Amaxe/Amaye/Amaze)

   e. Bo__es   (Boxes/Boyes/Bozes)

   f. Curl__   (Curlx/Curly/Curlz)

   g. Rela__   (Relax/Relay/Relaz)

   h. Monda__   (Mondax/Monday/Mondaz)

3. Write the names of at least six animals that you would see in a zoo:

   a. _____
   b. _____
   c. _____
   d. _____
   e. _____
   f. _____

Words to Remember

X — Xerox, X-mas, X-Ray, Xylophone

Y — yacht, yak, yam, yard, yarn, yawn, year, yeast, yell, yellow, yes, yesterday, yet, yolk, your

Z — zebra, zero, zigzag, zip, zoo

Date: _____   Teacher's Signature: _____

SPECIAL SOUND WORDS

We can create special sounds by putting certain letters together. These are called digraphs.

1. Read out the following:

    C + H = Ch
    S + H = Sh
    P + H = Ph
    W + H = Wh
    T + H = Th

    Now, match the objects with the sounds in their names:

    a. Th   i.

    b. Ph   ii.

    c. Sh   iii.

    d. Ch   iv.

    e. Wh   v.

2. Read out the following:

    C + R = Cr
    B + R = Br
    D + R = Dr
    F + R = Fr
    G + R = Gr

Teacher's Signature: _____   Date: _____

Now, fill in the blanks to discover the following sound words:

a. __ O W

b. __ E A D

c. __ I N K

d. __ U I T

e. __ A S S

3. Your teacher will read out the following paragraph. Underline all the special sund words and list them in the table given below:

Mani is Ramu's best friend. They share all their toys. Mani likes to play Chess. Ramu likes to draw. One day, Mani found a broken crayon hidden in the grass. "Who could have done this?" said Mani. He ran to Ramu's house and showed him the crayon. "Oh no!" said Ramu. "Now I can't colour my photo frame!" The boys told their parents what had happened. Ramu's mother got him a new box of crayons. The boys were happy again.

Th	Ch	Sh	Wh	Ph	Cr	Dr	Br	Gr	Fr

Date: _____   Teacher's Signature: _____

WORD POWER

1. Use the correct words to complete the following questions:

   > What   Why   Where   Who   How

   a. _____ are you going?

   b. _____ is that girl?

   c. _____ did you find her house?

   d. _____ are you crying?

   e. _____ is your name?

2. Name the four directions:

   a. E _ S _

   b. W _ _ T

   c. NO _ _ H

   d. S _ U _ H

3. Fill in the blanks by solving the jumbled words:

   > WINTER   UMBRELLA   SPRING   SUMMER

   a. We feel hot during _____ (MESUMR).

   b. It is very cold in _____ (RINTWE).

   c. We need an _____ (LLAUMRBE) during the rainy season.

   d. Pretty flowers grow in _____ (PINGRS).

Teacher's Signature: _____   Date: _____

4. Name the fruits and vegetables:

a.  _____

b.  _____

c.  _____

d.  _____

e.  _____

f.  _____

g.  _____

h. _____

Carrot

Apple

Brinjal

Pear

Potato

Banana

Tomato

Peas

5. Match the following:

a. One   7

b. Two   8

c. Three   5

d. Four   2

e. Five   9

f. Six   10

g. Seven   1

h. Eight   3

i. Nine   6

j. Ten   4

Date: _____   Teacher's Signature: _____

APPENDIX: SIGHT WORDS

Here are some words that we use very often. Learn a new word every day!

about	back	been	before	big
by	call	come	could	did
down	first	from	go	if
into	just	like	little	look
made	make	more	much	must
off	only	other	our	out
over	right	see	some	their
them	then	there	this	two
what	well	went	were	whom
when	where	which	who	your

Teacher's Signature: _____ Date: _____

ANSWER KEY

A and B

1.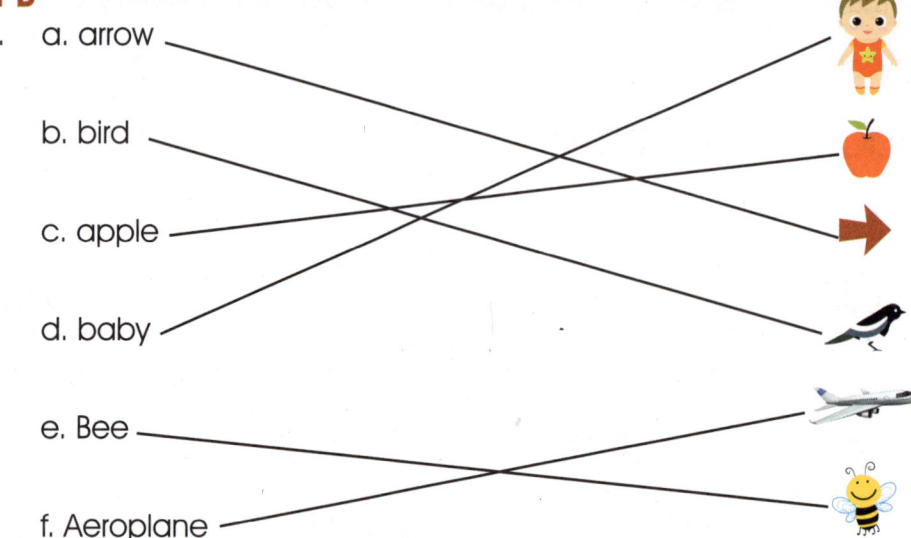
   a. arrow
   b. bird
   c. apple
   d. baby
   e. Bee
   f. Aeroplane

2. a. Bell   b. Ball   c. Ant   d. Artist
3. a. Blue   b. Arms   c. Bike   d. Ball   e. Age
4. a. Ape   b. Aeroplane   c. Boat   d. Brown

C AND D

1. a. Duck   b. Crow   c. Date   d. Drum   e. Cake   f. Cloud
   g. Doll   h. Car

2.

3. a. dog, calls   b. cup, cold

E AND F

1. a. Ear   b. Egg   c. Flag   d. Fish   e. Frog   f. Eye
2. a. Eat, Fat   b. Flag   c. Bed   d. Beat   e. Ever   f. Fog
   g. Bend   h. Lift
3. a. Five   b. Eight   c. Four
4. Eat, Ant, Heap, Tap, Tape, Heel, Pat, Pant

G AND H

1. a. Girl   b. Horse   c. Game   d. House   e. Hand   f. Grass
   g. Goat   h. Hair
2. a. house   b. green   c. hill   d. hug   e. grapes
3. a. horns   b. grass   c. hands   d. games   e. gifts
4. b. Gerl   c. Horce   f. Heal

Date: _____   Teacher's Signature: _____

I AND J

1. a. JAR   b. INK   c. JOB   d. IDEA   e. ISLAND
2.

I	I	C	I	C	L	E	I	I
G	N	L	R	N	L	E	I	V
L	K	J	E	L	L	Y	J	Y
O	P	J	L	U	D	J	O	W
O	O	A	A	J	D	A	K	J
J	T	I	N	S	I	D	E	U
E	N	L	D	J	D	E	R	G
T	J	A	W	J	A	M	O	I
I	S	L	A	N	D	J	E	O

3. a. MAGIC b. JACKET c. BIG d. LIKE e. JOKE f. JUMP
4. Joy, Full, Fully, You

K AND L

1. a. Lion   b. Knife   c. Kite   d. Lake   e. Key   f. King
   g. Lamp   h. Leg
2. a. Leaf   b. Leap   c. Kitten   d. Kiwi   e. Kid   f. Lame
3. a. Light, Kite   b. King   c. Lane   d. Long   e. Lit, Kit
   f. Leap, Keep   g. Lake   h. Life, Knife
4. a. kitten   b. lick   c. key   d. loaf   e. left   f. lungs

M AND N

1. a. MEAL   b. NECK   c. MILK   d. MASK   e. NINE
2. a. night   b. noon   c. nest   d. moon
3. a. MANGO   b. NOISE   c. NAIL   d. MOVIE
4. Male, Mat, Met, Meat, Meal, Metal, Melt, Lame, Tame, etc.

Teacher's Signature: _____   Date: _____

O AND P

1. Crossword:

   Down
   a. Orange
   b. Onion
   c. Paint
   d. Pig
   e. Oil

   Across
   c. Pencil
   d. Panda
   f. Owl

2. a. oxen   b. painter   c. pink, orange   d. paw   e. onions
3. a. PARK   b. OAR/PAR   c. PEAR   d. TAPE   e. NOT   f. BORN
   g. PATCH   h. FOOL

Q AND R

1.

2. a. quiet   b. rabbit   c. round   d. river   e. queen

3.
S	U	R	A	G	S	H	R
Q	R	I	B	S	L	Q	A
U	E	N	Q	I	Q	U	S
E	A	G	U	Q	U	I	H
S	L	T	R	S	I	E	S
T	I	Q	U	I	L	T	S
U	S	L	R	E	T	T	Q
R	E	A	D	I	N	G	Q

S AND T

1. S: Sea, Stars, Sun, Ship, Soap, Saw
   T: Tree, Top, Tank, Tent, Train, Torch

Date: _____   Teacher's Signature: _____

2. a. Seven Ships

   b. Ten Trees

   c. Six Swans

   d. Three Toffees

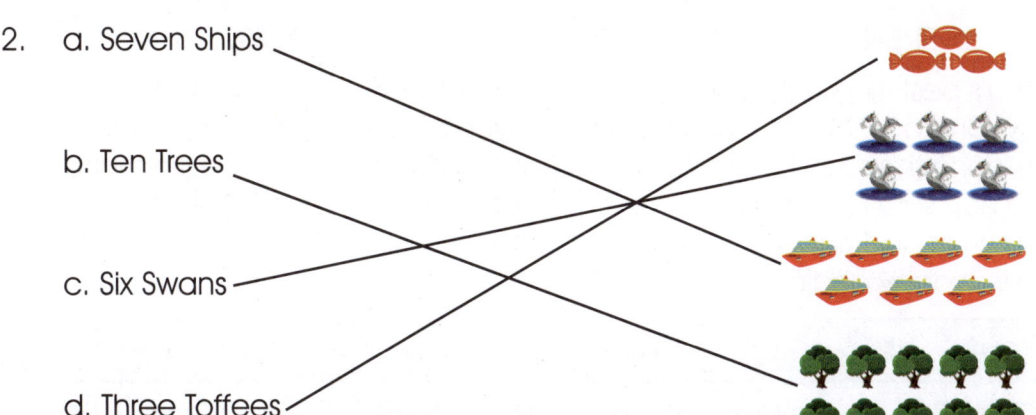

3. a. Sunshine: Sun, shine, shin, sin, shun, hen, nun, sis

   b. Transport: Port, top, ran, sport, tan, tap, pants, rat, torn, etc.

4. (Answers may vary)   a. TALL, TAIL   b. STEP, STAR
   c. TEST, TENT   d. THIS, THEN   e. SHIP, SHUT
   f. SEND, SEEN   g. TORN, TOPS

5. a. TIGER   b. TABLE   c. SUGAR   d. STOOL

U, V AND W

1. a. Umbrella   b. Vase   c. Watch   d. Vegetable   e. Web   f. Winter
   g. Uniform   h. Woman   i. Vulture   j. Uncle

2. a. wool   b. until   c. west   d. vase   e. under   f. valley
   g. visit   h. use   i. violin   j. water   k. vowels

X, Y AND Z

1. a. YACHT   b. ZEBRA   c. YOLK   d. X-MAS   e. ZIP   f. XEROX
   g. YELLOW   h. ZIGZAG

2. a. Exact   b. Every   c. Axe/Aye   d. Amaze   e. Boxes   f. Curly
   g. Relax/Relay   h. Monday

3. Lion, Zebra, Giraffe, Monkey, Tiger, Panda, Penguin, Snake, Rhino, etc.

SPECIAL SOUND WORDS

1. a. Th
   b. Ph
   c. Sh
   d. Ch
   e. Wh

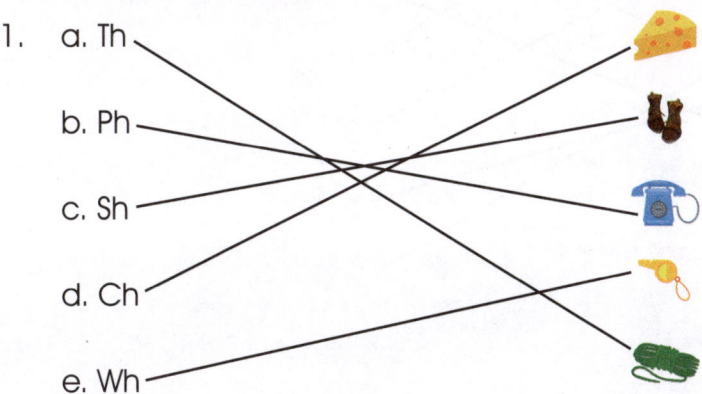

Teacher's Signature: _____   Date: _____

2. a. CROW   b. BREAD   c. DRINK   d. FRUIT   e. GRASS

3. Mani is Ramu's best <u>friend</u>. <u>They</u> <u>share</u> all <u>their</u> toys. Mani likes to play <u>Chess</u>. Ramu likes to <u>draw</u>. One day, Mani found a <u>broken</u> <u>crayon</u> hidden in <u>the</u> <u>grass</u>. "Who could have done <u>this</u>?" said Mani. He ran to Ramu's house and <u>showed</u> him <u>the</u> <u>crayon</u>. "Oh no!" said Ramu. "Now I can't colour my <u>photo</u> <u>frame</u>!" The boys told their parents <u>what</u> had happened. Ramu's <u>mother</u> got him a new box of <u>crayons</u>. <u>The</u> boys were happy again.

Th	Ch	Sh	Wh	Ph	Cr	Dr	Br	Gr	Fr
They	Chess	Share	Who	Photo	Crayon	Draw	Broken	Grass	Friend
Their		Showed	What						Frame
The									
This									
Mother									

WORD POWER

1. a. Where   b. Who   c. How   d. Why   e. What
2. EAST, WEST, NORTH, SOUTH
3. a. summer   b. winter   c. umbrella   d. spring
4. a. Apple   b. Carrot   c. Pear   d. Potato   e. Brinjal   f. Banana
   g. Peas   h. Tomato
5.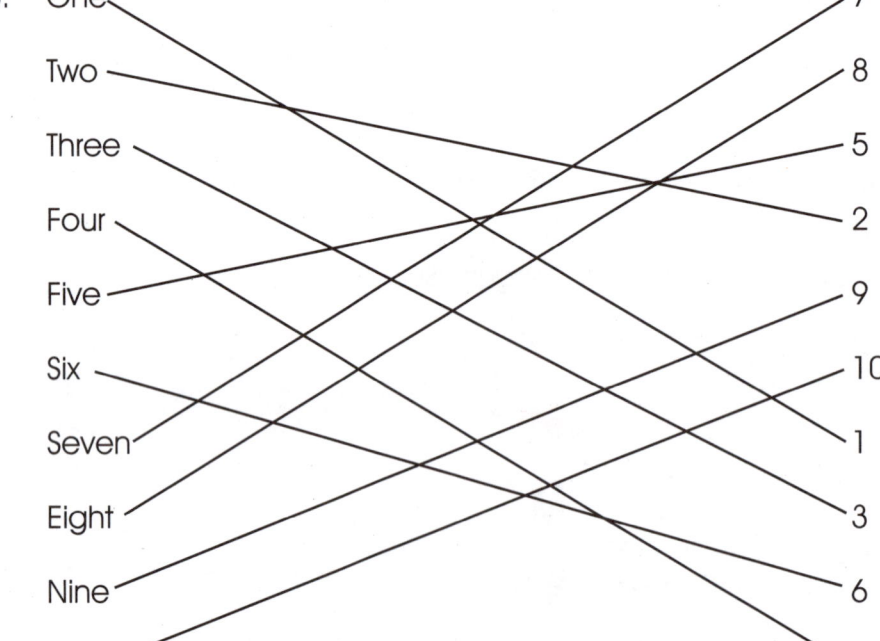